reflections

Seradin Veonne

BookLeaf
Publishing

India | USA | UK

Presentation by *BookLeaf Publishing*

Web: www.bookleafpub.com

E-mail: info@bookleafpub.com

ISBN: 978-93-5744-964-9

First edition 2022

DEDICATION

for Chelsie and for myself

ACKNOWLEDGEMENT

I acknowledge my elevated ancestors of blood and soul, for without them, I couldn't tell my story. I love you.
To Mommy, Daddy, Jason (Doom Twin One), Eli and My Honeydude, for your loving encouragement and keeping me full, and again Jason for your courage and inspiration. It's been a joy observing your process and evolution as an artist.
To Ian for being yourself unapologetically and making sure I completed this project.
To Bri and Malaika and all of the SLAP Collective who welcomed me with open arms.
To Timmie for sharing your heart and words with the world and for sharing the Slap Collective link in the first place. That one act saved my life.

in the mirror

strong yet subtle
born of lion and virgin, blood of the earth, red
and brown
hair that grows long as the deepest roots
breasts full of comfort
lips and thighs dipped in sugar and molasses
ass as big as a calabash, sis
a voice lush like velvet.
soft.
rich.
it glides
warm and cool.
a luxurious gift.
an embrace.
draped in lace, crimson lips
curls fall around my face
full hips
a slipper dangling off the lacquered toe
legs crossed at the knee
hem kissing the floor
always ready for more

music, mood

Headhunters, Vein Melter

slow and steady
languid
sensual
contemplative

sounds I love

babies laughter
ocean waves crashing
rain
bossa nova and samba
the moment you crack open a soda
bubble gum popping
the strike of a lighter
Teddy Pendergrass
Stevie Wonder
tuning forks
when the orchestra tunes together
biting into a pickle
wind blowing through the trees and leaves

adorn

My melanin
my hair in a fineapple
bold jewelry
lace and satin
red lip, dark lip
big ass shades
Versace fragrance
rose water
dresses w/pockets
mix match socks
heels, even if I only sit or lay down in em
freshwater pearls
scarves and long pieces of fabric

stardust

I am made of stardust.
You can see it in my smile
a smile appears on the mouth
is felt and seen on the eyes
and supports the crown
just like the star held in the night sky

Spring

Spring is my favorite season.
we emerge from winter, ready for rebirth,
renewal, rejuvenation, revelation.
the air smells different
the sun feels different
We can go outside again

flowers
pink purple peach
blooming
butterflies
flutter by
sparrows hopping
slightly off the ground
while we jump puddles
mindful of the earth worms

summertime is almost here
Springtime is beauty, joy, hope
growth life. another chance

what I love about myself

my smile
what my body feels when I really sing
how I fill out my clothes
my blerdiness
my lefthandedness
how hard my body works to protect
and keep me alive
my voice, especially when it has a lot of bass

my creative energy

it flows in cycles
some
days
it's
slow.
there are many days where there's a lot of
physical stillness but my mind is firing off like
firecrackers memorial day 2020.
other days, I'm able to bring it more into the
physical,
put it on paper, flesh it out, record it.

either way, I don't experience time at all.

the kiss

I'm glad I kissed you
on the cheek, I want your lips
glad I kissed you then

is it real this time?
have I tricked myself again?
do I really love you?

leisure, pleasure

laughing until the tears run
listening to the smell of rain
tasting sour things
beaches and sunbathing
watching cartoons
cuddling
talking to animals
singing at home
singing with a group
watching live bands

What do I need?

what do I need? and why are needs so
inconvenient?

when I need food, I have hunger.
when I need to release, I feel pressure.
when I need to move, I shake.
when I need to connect, I reach out.

when what I need is different than what is
expected, I am required to set a boundary. If I
don't I begin to feel resentment, literally to
"re-feel". I cannot let it go. Not establishing and
enforcing boundaries, creates a space where I
feel the pain of the unmet need, the regret of not
speaking up, self-betrayal and the missed
opportunity to protect my joy, my peace.

the biggest lie ever told

in a world where we are mainly seen
by how much we work,
how much we produce,
it's easy to think that our gifts,
our talents, our beauty, our genius,
our joy, our relaxation, our resources
and our rest are debts that must be paid for and
reconciled.

the biggest lie ever told, to get you to disconnect
from yourself and serve the machine.

You are deserving of your abundance.

Power

Power is waking up everyday, living to fight
another day.
Strength is the ability to not break down,
even if it means taking a break, asking for help
or simply walking away.
Holding on to yourself, instead of clasping to an
external thing.

Enough

Enough is enough. I am enough. I've given enough. I've done enough.

You don't have to keep proving yourself. You don't have to keep pushing. You are already deserving of the love, praise, admiration and accolade. There's been enough blood, sweat and tears to last throughout all the coming lifetimes.

Your Mama and Grandma was loyal enough. They sacrificed enough. They smiled to the world while wincing through the pain long enough. Your parents and ancestors worked themselves to the bone, offering up their breath and health and youth, and rest and dreams, of both day and night.

Bad backs, hips, knees, hearts, minds and teeth with no recompense, reparations or restitution given. Yellow paint in the street, added days on the calendar, bended knees, raised fists and shoulders draped with kente is what they think will suffice.
Now that, ain't enough.

intentions

what do I intend to do? what is the goal?
I've wandered aimlessly, pulled in different
directions
because there was no clear goal. or I forgot
about the goal.
Focus and Direct the energy.
where the energy goes, the power flows.

grow

"There's always room for improvement."

these 5 words
used to upset me as a child,
because I felt that it meant I wasn't good.
but if we don't learn, we don't adapt and evolve.
and if we don't grow, we stagnate and die.
just when we think we've seen it all, or done it
all,
we will always have an opportunity to learn,
to stretch ourselves and our minds.

how fast you go?

how fast you go?
I'm usually
cautious
like a toddler
taking
its
first
steps.

other times
I'm flying at breakneck speeds missing exits and
running reds through the streets

advice/chant

do something different this time
do something different this time
do something different this time
do something different this time
do something different this time
do something different this time
do something different this time
do something different this time
do something different this time
do something different this time
do something different

JOY

I feel joy in my chest
shoots up through my arms during a dance
to hug a loved one
give a high five
and at the same time joy
makes its way up through my chest
I gasp with excitement,
cheesing mad hard as the energy
makes my cheeks sit straight up
makes room for my teeth to show
makes room for my laughter and
all the shoutin' and carryin' on
I'm about to do

to my raw unadulterated self

for far far too long
I've behaved
refused to make waves
too scared to make a scene
I've valued others'
likes, wants and needs
more than my own
choked on my own
spit, snot, and blood
bones never picked
accepting things that were flung across the table
at me

No more
no more
no more self denial
no more self suppression
no more self sacrifice
no more lying to myself
no more

no more

reflection

sometimes,
I block the light when I'm afraid to shine myself.
but I want you to see your reflection.
can You see how beautiful You are?
feel how strong You are?
do You know your capacity?
I want You to see your reflection.

www.ingramcontent.com/pod-product-compliance
Lightning Source LLC
LaVergne TN
LVHW050304200726
843509LV00015B/3153